THE LISTENING CHAMBER

Arkansas Poetry Award Series

THE LISTENERS

poems

THE LISTENING CHAMBER
poems by William Aberg

The UNIVERSITY *of*
ARKANSAS PRESS
Fayetteville   1997

01   00   99   98   97   5   4   3   2   1

Designed by Alice Gail Carter

♾   The paper used in this publication meets the minimum
requirements of the American National Standard for Perma-
nence of Paper for Printed Library Materials   Z39.48-1984.

LIBRARY OF CONGRESS CATALOGING-IN-PUBLICATION DATA
Aberg, William, 1957–
    The listening chamber : poems / by William Aberg.
        p.   cm. — (Arkansas poetry award series)
    ISBN 1-55728-464-4 (c : alk. paper). — ISBN 1-55728-463-6
(p : alk. paper)
    I. Title.   II. Series.
PS3551.B376L5   1997
811'.54—dc21   97-942
                                                  CIP

to my friends, teachers, and family,
and especially my late father and grandfather

ACKNOWLEDGMENTS

There are problems inherent in preparing a manu-script in prison: the use of typewriters for other than legal work is expressly forbidden, poems are lost during transfer, and one can be months in finding someone with whom to share poetry.

I owe far more gratitude than I could ever repay and more to friends of years for their support, to men and women who namelessly stood by me in the twilight.

Several people deserve thanks for help with this project, including Richard Shelton, Lois Shelton, who typeset this manuscript from near-illegible pencil scrawls, and Pamela Stewart-Kothay, James Cervantes, and Leilani Wright, whose wise editing often clarified these pages.

I also would like to thank the editors and staff of the following magazines and journals in which some of these poems have appeared: *Alaska Quarterly Review,* "Vespertine"; *Chelsea,* "The Listening Chamber," "The Artist in Charcoal," and "The Sleepers"; *Contact,* "Note Left on the Bed"; *En Passant,* "The Remembering"; *Fortune News,* "Reductions"; *Mazagine,* "Collington Creek," "Barrio Anita 1983," and "Weddings"; *New Kauri,* "Exiles"; *Poetry,* "Cymbeline"; *Prison Writing Review,* "The Old Romance"; *Sonora Review,* "Grey Figures"; *The Lucid Stone,* "Your Lap"; *The Sun,* "Winter in Maryland"; *Thunder Mountain Review,* "Romantic Firewood"; *Walking Rain Review,* "Evening, '74," "En Passant," "Bicycle Messenger," "My Real Mission," "Au Revoir," and "Devotions."

"The Old Romance" and "Romantic Firewood" appeared in the chapbook *The Lark and the Emperor,* published by Bits Press, Case Western Reserve University.

"Grey Figures," "Philosophies of the Dusk," "The Listening Chamber," and "A Penitent's Dream of Venus" (as "The Harvest") appeared in the chapbook *Philosophies of the Dusk* published by Moon Pony Press, Tucson. "A Penitent's Dream of Venus" also was published in the anthology *Light from Another Country*, edited by Joseph Bruchac, Crosscultural Press.

"Devotions," "Au Revoir," "Bicycle Messenger," "En Passant" and "My Real Mission" are forthcoming in the anthology *Contemporary Arizona Poets*, edited by Leilani Wright and James Cervantes, University of Arizona Press.

"Reductions" received the P.E.N. Muriel Rukeyser Award in 1983.

CONTENTS

PART THREE

When taken out of context, as it often is, W. H. Auden's line "poetry makes nothing happen" is difficult for me to accept. Although I admire Auden's work extravagantly, I am always looking for the poem by somebody —anybody—that will change a life or save a river or prevent a war, and of course I'm constantly disappointed. But this first volume of poetry by William Aberg—Billy to everyone who knows him—has made me pause to reconsider. Perhaps I have been looking for the action, for the miracle, at the wrong end of things.

Because I know something about how and where and under what circumstances these poems were written, I am aware that they have made something happen. They have saved the poet's life. The writing of them has kept him alive when he would otherwise be dead. I am not speaking figuratively.

Nor is it an accident that many of the poems in *The Listening Chamber* deal with transcendence. In one of them, the poet, who was a bicycle messenger in Washington, D.C., for several years, describes a three-second chance encounter at a stoplight between a bicycle messenger and a beautiful woman. The messenger is so filled with euphoria that he looks up at the impending storm clouds and says, "Let me have it!" In another poem, when light from a window touches his lover's breasts, it is enough to create in the poet "awe that goes beyond language."

Even as I am aware that many of these are poems of transcendence, I am appalled at the suffering which went into the writing of them and the snake-pit depths of misery from which many of them came. Some of them were written in a state mental hospital, some in a county jail, some in a state prison, some in a federal prison, some in a halfway house for addicts, and some in what we call the free world, although I doubt that any of them were written by a man who was entirely free.

I doubt that Billy Aberg has ever been really free. He is in prison as I write this, and I cannot speak for the future. In the words of Michael Hogan, another fine American poet who wrote some of his best work in prison, I have learned "not to expect too much or believe too strongly." That's from one of Hogan's poems, quite aptly called "Love," written from the Arizona State Prison in the mid-1970s. Both Billy and Michael were my "students" at different times, yet I laugh out loud when the irony strikes me of how little they learned from me and how much I learned from them, and continue to learn.

Years ago, before his father's death, I spent the night with Billy's family in Maryland, and one of his sisters told me something I have never been able to get out of my mind. "When Billy was young" she said, "even before he was a teenager, his need to gain the acceptance of his friends was so great he would do anything."

I thought about the astronaut on the tether in space, the tether that has been cut by a wicked robot/computer. He drifts away, becoming smaller and smaller, and no one can hear his cries for help. Watching that process over the years, and watching Billy's frantic attempts, again and again, to pull himself back into hailing distance of the spaceship containing all he knows of love, I have come to realize there are many kinds of exile, and many kinds of prisons.

Recently when I was talking to his mother on the phone, she said, "Billy would be such a terrific person if he just weren't a manic-depressive, alcoholic, drug addict." She spoke with great love, and she was serious. All this is true. Yet reading his poetry, I am left in wonder—wonder that he has survived, that he can love and need so fiercely, that he continues to write, that he can tell the truth in his poems (perhaps only in his poems), that his talent is so great, that his work embodies an awareness of poetry spanning many centuries and many cultures, and that he can very ably represent, in spite of his youth, a literary tradition that extends back to the beginnings of poetry in the English language.

He is the outsider, the exile. He is neither the warrior nor the intellectual, although he might envy both of them. He is the artist. Something happened to him in the womb or before that. He does not know what, but he lives in a chemical maelstrom, flying up and then down and finding whatever he can of stability in the love sometimes offered to him. Most of all, I am in wonder that the writing of his poems, the record of his exile, has been his means of survival. I view the poetry, itself, with wonder. It is beautiful, it is painful, and it has made something happen.

And what about his life? I see his life as if a Greek tragedy had begun to drag out its inevitable and relentless horror in my kitchen. His life goes on somehow. I can do nothing about his life, although I have tried in the past. Both my wife and I have, one at a time, sat in front of a jury and tried to convince them that on a certain night when Billy had dinner with us he was insane, and we did help to convince them, in order to buy him a year in the state mental hospital rather than another long sentence in prison. Even then he spent more than a year in the state hospital, and at the end of his time there the federal system intervened and he was sent to a federal prison, where he is still incarcerated, although expecting release soon.

Ultimately I can do nothing about his life. I can only react to the tragedy, and wonder at the poetry. What is it Aristotle says about how we react to tragedy? Pity and fear, fear and pity. Also horror, hopelessness, and despair. And guilt, always plenty of guilt. Those of us who love Billy, as my wife and I do, go through it all, as if a light show were playing over our psyches. The only light that seldom goes on for us in this situation is the light of hope.

But Billy has hope. It illuminates his work. He goes on, rising and falling, falling and rising, on the same bipolar roller coaster he has ridden most of his life; but he has chosen hope. When something good happens, even a chance word from a pretty young woman he will never see again or a peaceful summer evening in an often violent *barrio*, he celebrates it, as we all should, but most of us do not because we take such things for granted. Billy has learned to take nothing for granted. The rope he walks is too narrow for that. He celebrates life every day that he manages to live it.

For several reasons, some of which are technical while others have to do with his attitudes and choice of subjects, Billy's poems remind me of the painting of the Dutch genre painters of the seventeenth century, such as Gabriel Metsu, Jan Steen, and especially Johannes Vermeer. The technical reasons are most obvious. The poet's loving attention to the details of texture and color are everywhere. "The sky / an orange liquor / over the coming dark, a woman / brushing twigs from her hair, / dwarf trees sparkling / with a lavender mist." The lingering care and delight with which he paints a scene makes everything, including the setting, beautiful, in spite of the fact that something horrible might be taking place or that the situation is tawdry and pitiful.

Another technical quality of the poetry that makes me think of those glowing genre paintings is Billy's treatment of light. He is, in fact, a poet of light. Like the genre painters, he usually manages to get a source of light into the poem, rather than merely illuminating his subject from without. But his sources of light, unlike the lamps and open windows in the genre paintings, are often small, flickering, and ironic.

In the richly detailed setting of a Roman Catholic church, his mother lights a candle and prays that he will never come home again. In the same poem he lights a match beneath the addict's spoon. There is still warmth, light, and comfort in these small flames, but they illuminate hopelessness and pain, as if to underscore the fact that he is writing from the fag-end of the twentieth century, not the mid-seventeenth.

One of the most unusual of his uses of light is in "Collington Creek," a poem based on one of his several suicide attempts. He foresees himself dying on the bank of the creek and "the light burning like phosphorus / around the outline of my body" as time passes and he becomes part of the earth.

Few contemporary poets can manipulate light with the care and effectiveness of this one. Many of us, it would seem, don't even try. These poems glow from within, although that light often comes from a tiny flicker or a drug-induced warmth. His surfaces come to life with texture and color from the play of light upon them, and the dreadful becomes even more dreadful in such a rich, luminous world.

Like the genre painters, this poet also knows how to portray human flesh and especially the human face and to view his subjects in the everyday settings which show them to best advantage. "Stepping Away from My Father" shows all of this going on at once. The poet's father, a government employee, is sending a long, friendly message by telegraph to one of his counterparts in Siberia. The father's face "is warm, animate, / his lips silently forming the words / he taps out in code. . . ." Beneath this the poet sees a more typical genre picture. "This could be / the conversation of two men in a local / hardware store, arms folded across their chests / as they stand beside the snow shovels and salt sacks. . . ." At the end, the young poet, who has been waiting by the door to ask his father for a loan, backs out quietly, not wanting to recognize "the fear in his eyes when he sees his addict son."

It's all there in one short poem: the richness of texture and detail, the feeling of real, breathing people in their ordinary settings, their warm, lovingly presented faces, and the wrenching knowledge that it is all gone and will never come back again. As the Brazilian poet Carlos Drummond de Andrade captured life in the Western World before World War I in a single aching line—"They had gardens, they had mornings in those days"—this poet paints the world beautiful because he knows it is lost to him. He writes, always, from exile.

When all of these various elements of the poet's talent are brought to bear on a love poem, the result can be unforgettable. "Meeting in South Tucson" is an unlikely candidate for the love-poem classification, but it is a love poem nonetheless. The poet is on his way to buy drugs in an unsavory neighborhood when he encounters a young woman on the same errand, but she is being shadowed by a police car and asks the poet to pose as her lover so it will look as if she is meeting him instead of attempting to buy drugs. After the police have gone, the couple find the drugs they are searching for in a run-down "aluminum Airstream" with a "milk-crate step." Because her other veins are destroyed from drug use, the girl exposes "a small Latin breast" and asks the poet to find a vein there. For this intimate moment they have cleared "a patch / of rug among some dirty jackets" on the trailer floor. Later, she writes her name in ink on his wrist so he will not forget her. At any rate, the reader is not likely to forget this chance meeting between two addicted children in Hell.

I am not good at chasing literary influences affect-ing the work of contemporary poets, nor do I think it is a particularly worthwhile pursuit. It is easy to find what one is looking for. But in this case the situation is too curious and significant for me to resist. Here is a young American poet who has not pursued an M.F.A. degree and has spent much of his life incarcerated in one way or another, but who has managed to read widely. The literary influences that one can see most obviously and that the poet admits quite readily are nearly all European. Billy admits to having been greatly impressed by many French poets, both surrealists and postsurrealists.

All writers have literary antecedents, and those poets are lucky who have been able to choose theirs wisely and well. In Billy's case, the choice of a major technical influence was probably intuitive, like falling in love, but it was brilliant.

It was brilliant because the choice made it possible for Billy to absorb techniques developed to describe and re-create one kind of world and then apply them to a quite different kind of world. This sets up a tension in Billy's work that gives it energy and resilience. The reader sees horror through the eyes of innocence. The poet I am referring to is the French judge Jean Follain (1903-1971). Follain's poetry is a series of delicate and hauntingly lovely portraits of life in the tiny French village of Canisy remembered from his childhood. He was sent away to school in Paris during his adolescence, and from that point on, as a poet, he wrote about a world he no longer inhabited, re-creating again and again some small scene from his beloved village.

It might be considered strange that a young addict in prison in the American Southwest owes so much as an artist to a French judge born near the turn of the century. One could make much, I suppose, of the fact that both of them have been deeply involved with the law, but the joke is too grim for me to pursue it. The situation has a surreal tinge, but I can think of nothing more surreal than the American prison system today.

Jean Follain probably comes closer than any other modern poet to accomplishing in words what the Dutch genre painters accomplished in their paintings. He presents his scenes of everyday life in Canisy without editorial comment, but with such attention to color, texture, and detail that they continue to resonate in the reader's mind. What strikes the reader of Follain's work, beyond its incredible technical facility, is the purity and innocence of his vision. He sees the complexity and irony of his world, but all the rough edges are smoothed by his memory, and everything glows as if lighted by the setting sun.

I can think of many reasons why Billy Aberg

would be attracted to the work of this French poet who died about twenty-five years ago. Both poets write from a sense of exile; and in spite of all he has seen and done, there is an innocence and gentleness about Billy and about the way he sees the world. It makes him appealing as a person and gives his poetry a marked tension, making it unforgettable, as if the crack houses and prisons of America were being seen through the eyes of a child.

I guess it is too late in the twentieth century to try to hide anything, and it probably always was. So here is my friend Billy Aberg with all his warts and bruises as well as his innocence and gentleness—a man who prizes life but keeps trying to kill himself, a man who values his freedom strongly but spends most of his time in one kind of prison or another, a man whose life is as contradictory and bizarre as the times he lives in. It's impossible to say whether his talent is in spite of all this or because of all this but, at any rate, he is a damned good poet.

RICHARD SHELTON
Tucson — October 19, 1996

ONE

THE BLADE

for William Stafford

As a boy, I made a blade
of my hand and held it
flush with the window
of our speeding car.

Telephone poles, great
windy chestnuts and oaks, tall
buildings, and green, bearing slopes—
I leveled them all exactly in my wake.

One day, I fear
I'll have to live in that country.

THE LISTENING CHAMBER

Don't wait to be hunted to hide.

Whoever is out to get me
can find me lying

under the bed
of this project apartment,
ear to the floor,
shotgun lined heart-level
at the door,
an engraved derringer
snug in my back pocket.

I've practiced
the art of anonymity
for years: one blue eye
flickering over my shoulder,
hat brim shadowing
half of my face.

They won't find me
an easy target: I have more
faces than an actor
and I'm less conspicuous.

They don't need a reason
to dog my every step—
it would only slow them down.

To have done nothing
worth punishment
is to eliminate my reason for living—
I've done something
I'm afraid of being caught for.

THE ARTIST IN CHARCOAL

for René Magritte

A man in a black bowler—let's call him X—is reading a daily news-paper by the town fountain when a woman with long, dark hair, and skin the color of suet unslings her purse and sits beside him, Pulling a small sketch pad from her bag, she begins to draw his picture.

X fumbles for the cigarettes in his suit pocket, taps one out and lights it, his fingers trembling. He's never seen the woman before, and her face is all the more startling because she has glass eyes. With her right hand she traces his lips, nose and cheekbones; with her left she draws and shades.

Excuse me, Ma'am, says X, but haven't you mistaken me for someone else? His tone is that of a man pressed to the limits of courtesy.

You're the same as anyone, she replies. X tries gently but firmly to rise, but she stays him with her hand. With the other she moves aside her pad and bag, wrinkles her forehead, and eases out one eye, pressing it into his shaking hand.

Take a look at yourself with it, and maybe you'll see yourself the way I do, she says and begins to laugh.

X panics, tosses the eye into the lapfolds of her skirt and takes off down the boulevard, his heels clattering on the cobblestones.

Holding the grey eye aloft in the sunlight, she turns the pupil toward the world.

PARENTHESIS

If it weren't for his voice—a husky
Spanish octave below my own—I could almost pretend
our bench sat in the musk of spring grass,
by slender, flowering cherry trees and dogwoods,
and instead of a dry prison field
in rifle range of Mexico, this was a park
surrounded by brownstone houses
whose walls are spidered with ivy,
and this fragile young man, his cheeks
faintly rouged by red pencil, eyebrows plucked
and darkened, could be the woman
in flesh his spirit longs to flower into,
and it could be twilight, with dinner and a movie ahead,
and we could lock fingers with the easy grace of lovers
long together, for a change
two people delighted by what is
rather than what could be. So lost am I in this
for a moment I reach to clasp his hand.

NOCTURNE

For V. Shalamov

Lacing my boots
on the barracks steps
near the end of a sleepless
Siberian night, I look up

in time to see
a shooting star vanish
in an orange shower of sparks.

Another light
gone, another thing
that will never again challenge
my certainty of the dark.

A PENITENT'S DREAM OF VENUS

He had assigned to that same lady more
Than it is proper to concede to mortals
—LUCRETIUS

The thighs were awkward at first—
stiff blue denim.
But he stuffed each leg with rags and towels
and primped them
until they were firm enough
to hold his weight. The breasts posed
a bigger problem: tangerines
felt too small and hard, and rolled
unmercifully. So he skipped them over,
pretending she was young
and eager for heat. Still, something
seemed missing, perhaps an intimate
voice, the warm springiness
of muscle and bone.

But he wouldn't give up
trying, though
through the cell window
the guard shone his flashlight
on the white, rising
slopes of his buttocks, laughed,
and moved along.
And though he wrought nothing
from his clumsy attempts
at passion, a certain warmth
like release
flared in his abdomen,
and he drew up the blanket
around both of their shoulders.
But when he pulled out
the rumpled rags and towels
damp with sweat, something inside him

fell apart, too,
and he sat for a moment
nude on the bed,
tried to reassemble her, but couldn't,
and lay down with the empty jeans
and shirt in his hands, created
the rest of her body
with his eyes. And often
during the night, she spoke to him
in a voice airy and gentle as goosedown—
so quietly, he could understand
no words, simply a sound
like the rhythm of water
under the pale tide of the moon.

ROMANTIC FIREWOOD

A man is   chopping the moon for firewood
in the forest   near my house
There is blood   on his face
and hands   Like most he sees the moon as
a graveyard for   listless romantics
The small   headstones are falling

A man is falling near   my headstone
Like most he sees   the graveyard
as a listless moon   In the forest
the romantics are chopping   his small face and hands
for firewood   there is blood on the house

and moon A romantic   man is
chopping firewood   on the moon Like most
he sees his house   as a graveyard for falling head-
stones There are small faces   in the forest
near the moon   listless hands in my blood

PHILOSOPHIES OF THE DUSK

Some keep their lamps burning
all night, fueled
by the red oil of nerves
and insomnia: theirs
is the desire to keep things
visible, where
they can be named
or avoided. My room is

not one of those. I like
the dusk. To look
at the pile of clothes
lying on my bed
and think, It could be
a woman there
sleeping. Or to look
at the woman
sleeping there
and think, It could be
dirty laundry I left
on the bed. A lamp

can prove things, dispel
myth. I prefer
the suggestions of the twilight
through the window, the play
of shadows and sky,
the door to the theatre
of possibilities
which awaits only dark to define it.

THE SLEEPERS

They are sleeping: dreams came to them while they toiled in the fields, and they unstrapped their plows, dropped their hoes, and plodded past the stone fences to the roads that led them home.

Each man pulled back his blanket, fluffed his pillow, crawled under the sheets and went to sleep.

What their dreams are no one can discover: the windows of their houses are blind with steam, and their walls and roofs expand and contract like women in labor.

But each morning, before sunrise, another patch of the fields has been harvested without anyone visible to work the earth, without anyone to taste its profits.

DELUSIONS OF GRANDEUR

The insecurities of the prison cell
keep me awake. It longs to be a large, genteel
apartment with French doors,
a balcony with a view
to the Eiffel Tower or Champs Élyseés,
where artists and emigrés
scoop caviar and paté
on cucumber slices and crackers
with white wine or champagne,
and ballerinas from the Kirov talk
of tours to Montreal and New York.
                    Look at these walls,
it moans. *Cinder block!*
they should be clean and white,
ready for some of Monet's Water Lilies
perhaps, or a Renaissance odalisque
in oil. And to put a toilet
and sink in the room where you sleep! Sinks
should be porcelain, not steel, host
to lipstick cartridges and rouge,
bottles of eau de cologne, atomizers of perfume,
not slivers of lye soap and a state toothbrush.
Mon Dieu! And your bunk
must have been designed for the Inquisition,
the way you twist and fidget.
It is an impoverished place indeed
that women do not visit.

I reassure it as best I can
that even nobility knows hard times,
and console its dramatic soul
with a cassette of Pavarotti's arias,
and follow with Vivaldi's *Four Seasons*,
until all I hear from the walls and ceiling
is the rhythm of shallow breathing.
Tiptoeing to my bunk, I stuff my ears

with cotton balls and close my eyes—
I, too, need my sleep:
I promised my cell that tomorrow
I would read to it from *Paradise Lost.*

–

APOLOGY TO CONGRESS AFTER VISITING
THE CAPITAL STAIRS WITH MY DOG BECKETT

I'm sorry: my dog was responsible for the lump
of waste which sat mute and graceless on the steps
untold hours in the September heat, and although
in past months he's refrained, having been trained well,
squatting only in discrete byways of earth and grass
or on paper, as circumstance allowed, something
about the gleam of the old marble stair,
the fluted Corinthian columns and marvelous dome
must have caused his intestines to stir—in thrill—
and like the architect, engrossed over his prints,
inspired him also to create a monument, to leave
a brief signature of his passage through life.
I'm sure you will view this with compassion
in your high, white office, understanding that
when unable to express appreciation in private,
to leave one's respects at the door, must often suffice.

THE PRIMACY OF ODOR

Nearing dawn, as I unzip
to piss, the new cat
leaps to the porcelain lip
of the bowl, face
intent on the heavy stream,
the tinted swirl
and roar of the flush.

What an incredible world,
his eyes tell me
as he jumps
back to the tile,
escorts me down the hall
to the living room couch,

where, curling
beside my thigh on the cushion,
he nudges at my newspaper
with his head.
I scratch under his chin
with my nails, feeling
honored, somehow,
wishing this trust
I could equal with any man.

MY REAL MISSION

Sometimes they ask me how I put
the mayonnaise on the table, let alone
milk or bread. I touch my fingers to my lips
and point to a set of blueprints
open on the desk. *Don't let this get around,*
I tell them, *but those belong to the Mexican Navy:
it's the diagram of the world's first adobe submarine.*
And if doubt curls their eyebrows
or lips, I point to my frog mask and fins
to prove my passion for sinking.

Sometimes I even reveal
facets of the truth: how life as a bona fide
medical experiment entitles me free hours
to patrol the cosmos, drink
mead with Aphrodite on Mt. Olympus,
and pour vinegar in the goblets of the gods.
And more. But by and large I mumble
something humble, how if I were more worthy
I might be a broker on Wall Street,
a welder, or a lawyer. Yet my eyes

shine as I say it. I have the balls
to repeat that I have seen
tiny glimpses of eternity beyond the city lights,
here, over the mountains, something
at the edge of vision. It hasn't ruined me.
I mean, I'm still impressed.
Dinner with wine and hors d'oeuvres
will never distract me again.

TWO

WEDDINGS

Mornings, when the first
gold threads
wrap the trees, I sense
the light those strands withhold—
this is poetry: separating
each thread gently
with both thumbnails
until the light of the visible
blends with the light of the invisible.
Through this bright web
the fly extends its tiny, upturned hands.

COLLINGTON CREEK

November. The cattails rise, brown
and feathery from the twilight marsh,
and between fallen trees, peppered
by rot, evening pools
reflect the bright thumbnail
of a crescent moon.

Venus, tiny
white ball of fire, moves
slowly beyond a storm-
cracked locust,
and from the banks
of the creek, a muskrat
slips into water, its head
dividing the surface
as it swims toward its lodge
of branches and mud.

If I can keep quiet
long enough,
if on this damp
black mattress of soil
I can maintain my balance,
the light burning like phosphorus
around the outline of my body
might dissolve into the darkening
beeches and elms, the cirrus
cool water, and constellations,
the deep clairvoyant air
which joins together all things.

THE REMEMBERING

Evening pulls in its brown quills
tipped with fire, the moon
climbs to autumn's stage, never
unwanted, unblessed.
White cheese and fresh bread
arrayed on the quilt, your hair
lighting the paper birches, we sit
in this woodland theatre, your fingers
warming my skin, your blouse
open, one hand cupping
your chin. The stream spills
its water down moss and black rock
behind us: this world we dream of
dreams us, who—restored—
lie fading between trees, two
lights among lights
in the abandon of the world.

VESPERTINE

I can still see it, evenings: the sky
an orange liquor
over the coming dark, a woman
brushing the twigs from her hair,
dwarf trees sparkling
with a lavender mist. But it's
something else, a step
into the old, wonderful story
in which the stars have yet to appear.

In this, her hip
sways under my hand
and I love it, want the walk
home to be farther: the footpath,
maple-eaved, unwinds
through the forest, up hills
lithe with birch
and poplar, down slopes
of laurel and sassafrass
into a gulley where the leaves
lie black with dew. This

is the walk of dreamers,
the vast, patient wood
where we turn
toward each other, everything
so delightfully
unclear, her small shoes
edging up to my own,
one in the light,
one in the dark, the way
a balance of two belongs.

THE OLD ROMANCE

after Miklos Radnoti

Under the bright moon   on old porches
the romance goes on   and we are not there
to embrace it   Turn away   how
can you enjoy   its fire
without us?   Maybe it will be
there if we return   Our fingers lie to us
in the night   tell us we are beautiful
wanted like new clothes   I wish they were here
calling our names   But this moment   is all we have
the slightest movement   in the corridor
frightens us away   the loaded rifles
Do women   call for us
when loving others   even think of us?
Our lives   go on without us
and we are left   calling them back
like lost dogs   Who will
remember our voices   while in two lives
we dream on steel bunks   work in wasted fields

CYMBELINE

Tonight, roses flame in the blue vase
by her bed, and the stuffed bear
she once held to her printed dress
sits high on the shelf, lifeless
white wool. You clatter open the shutters
and the wind sings through to fill your body
artery to vein, shoulder to hand
as the clock's slow arm turns dawn
to a bright transfusion of blood
on sky. For a time, grief forgets you

and the child reaches through
its snow-banked walls into emptiness,
her voice rising through the winter lawn
like strata escaping the ground,
while your memories lace fog
around the bare linden and oak,
trickle light down your throat
as your neighbors pick up milk
from crates on the stoop, retreat

into their houses as the spokes
of her bike crumple again
into the grille of a station wagon
skidding down the street
on black ice. And the young girl
spiraling onto the lawn: how
she folds her arms so gracefully,
as if in the sculptured air of remembrance
she were swathing an angel in the snow.

YOUR LAP

It is a haven, this
warm, pelvic cradle where
I prop my head, each moment
more content, more ignorant
of obligation as you rest
the spine of a novel
against my cheek

and read me,
in a soft voice
about the ending of exile,
about one man
who, against all laws
of literature, returns
stronger and happier,
to his family and home.

Tonight, I feel
every dolt walking the earth
should have, like this,
a lap, a warming place
to lose the noise
of the street and bathe
in the glow rising up
from a hearth of muscle
and bone. Here,

as we braid our fingers
and let our hands
release their cold,
I can forget the crackling
ache of the walls
for fresh paint, the awful
dying hues of the lawn,

and hear, nearby
in your pulse, the rumor

of deep, fluent streams
winding through lilies and ferns,
where the day loses velocity
and gathers me into
this bright, feminine lake
lit by silent trees and sky.

NOTE LEFT ON THE BED

A thin stripe of windowlight divides
your breasts as you sleep,
and I lie, one eye
open, on my elbow, watching you
from across a tiny sea
of sheets, thinking: only in silence
could anybody be this perfect—
the closed petals
of your vagina, dimly
pink, show from the soft pelt
of your parted thighs,
and your stomach, almost
mauve in the dusk air, rises
and falls in rhythm
with your breath, your eyes
and cheeks half obscured
by shadow and hair.
Here, the heat from your sleeping frame
kindles a musk, an abdominal ache
that fills my muscles
with blood. But it isn't simple
want of sex awakens me
to watch you, but a lack of faith
in talk, a need to express
this awe that goes beyond language
or thought, a desire to bask
in this reverie
sparked by a plain love
of your presence, this trust
that asks my body to speak.

AU REVOIR

Adiós, Arrivederce,
old trailer courts overgrown
with oleander, alleys crunching gravel
and glass under the tire
of squad cars. Legs, lungs: no longer
do you need tighten to run

that one crucial kilometer
in slow, arroyo sand, dodge Dobermans
and pit bulls to escape the cops,
Bloods, Crips, or whoever
they are after me
with automatic weapons and knives.

Goodbye, good riddance,
dismayed and outraged citizens: I'm off
to the Big Yonder. Someone else
will have to fudge with his fly by the dumpster,
or heave in the half-step of the Lowlife
Serenade. So long, *mi vida loca,*

it was never sweet, but I have to leave
now: you have eaten both my feet
          and still you are hungry.

DEVOTIONS

It's too easy
to describe: the match flame
charring the spoon, the blown veins,
the ravenous ghost who throws stolen
gold and gems into a lake
of pain that ripples
out in circles to everything

it loves. I remember
now, in April, the old chapel
on a hill of mountain laurel, windy
maple and oak, grass
speckled white with dogwood blossom—
there, in the flickering red

scent of the votive cups,
my mother genuflects and turns to kneel
under the feet of the Virgin, slips
some coins in a box, and prays,
lighting a wick in my name, that I might find
healing, keep healthy, have enough
to eat. That I know how much

she loves me. But that I never come home again.

STEPPING AWAY FROM MY FATHER

My father leans toward the green, electric
dials of the transceiver, clicking the Morse key
between thumb and forefinger, talking in dashes and dots
with a man in Magadan, far
eastern Siberia, about how they put fire pots
all night beneath running truck engines to keep the gas
and oil from freezing. How the Sea of Okhotsk,
even now, in late March, is a plateau
passable only in the wake of icebreakers.
My father tells him how an early Maryland spring
has teased the flowers and trees into a bloom
that could still be murdered
by frost. This could be
the conversation of two men in a local
hardware store, arms folded across their chests
as they stand beside the snow shovels and salt sacks
and grouse about insurance, doctor's bills,
the motions of clouds and sun.
My father's face is warm, animate,
his lips silently forming the words
he taps out in code, the signals
flashing over the Atlantic, the skies of Europe,
over the snowy steppe and taiga of Holy Russia.
I, who have stood by the door
waiting to ask for a loan, back quietly
into the hall, not wanting to startle him
out of his easier intimacy with strangers, nor sense
the fear in his eyes when he sees his addict son.

EN PASSANT

Help me remember: I am a visitor here
at these monk-like tables, circled by a sect of blue
chambray and denim, where an alert violence—
concealed lightning—passes the room

eye to eye. Remind me that these crossed, muscular
forearms, these striated biceps livid with tattoos
will lose tone in years. Do not let me forget:
let me laugh with a friend, work with a rake

or pick, relaxed but aware how the damp
spots—fear—can mushroom under the armpits
when I stare through the fence at the crescents
of snow on the mountain peaks in the December air

and realize that no card or letter has arrived
in weeks and I haven't noticed, or cared. If the bunk
and meals are enough, remind me again that I'm a traveler here:
and if I plod the yard, unaware of the desert rain,

or the tiny pinhole—Venus—through a lavender cloud,
the scent of creosote after a storm, slap me awake.
Strike me if my skin turns grey, if I grow immune
to loss or pain. Under the stairwell, show me the blade

if, worse, my eyes do not laugh with my lips and days
lapse to a haze, fixing *chiva* on soda cans. Here,
too, is life—no charade—but I want a fire in this skin
to remember the cardinal sin: not to love freedom enough.

THREE

REDUCTIONS

now living is all that is left
the simple test of endurance
—SUSAN NORTH

Afternoons, in this plague
of flies and white, Sonoran heat, we rarely sing—
to be honest, not
at all. The porter unrolls the hose
and waters the dirt to keep it from blowing
up in our faces when the southern winds
hit. Crouched on the walk
outside our cells, we keep busy
lying about what we would do
if a woman appeared
to us, her lips a coarse violet,
wanting each one of us

right now. Or how easily
we could distract the guard
from his perch on the guntower—
one fake fight
and we might make it
over the fence before the count
officer found us missing. I remember
one cynic, locked up
twelve years, spat tobacco
in a paper cup, pushed up the brim
of his cap, and told us

the jagged range
of mountains outside the prison
fence marked the edge
of the world, and the sky
was simply a revolving backdrop
someone painted with clouds
and stars. We laughed,
but for him, it was truth:
there could be no other world.

EVENING, '74

A friend once asked me to split
his tooth with a hammer and flathead
screwdriver so he could con a doctor
with night hours for a script of morphine.
I didn't have the stomach
and refused: his frail, peroxide
girlfriend scowled at me as she picked
up the tools and halved his molar to the gums.
They're nuts, I thought. Half the night
they went from clinic to hospital, simply
to return, nodding and triumphant,
to burn more holes in the couch
with their Marlboros. This
was an early year, before
I knew the line between desire and need.

SIEMPRE

She tells me through the vent
from the cell below
that they're taking her
on the morning train to the *pinta*,
that the guards have already packed
everything but her sheets,
blue jumpsuit, and towel.

Through the floor,
with my heart as with an eye,
I can see her as she sits
on the bunk, face
cupped in her hands,
elbows propped on her thighs,
cheeks smudged by fingermarks
and tears, her dark
hair eclipsing her knees.

I try to reassure her
with wisdom I do not have,
and hope I try to fake,
that the hammer
and anvil of coming days
will forge us into
something stronger.

By the time they unlock
my cell at breakfast,
she has already gone. But later
as I walk back in my boxers
from the shower, an older guard,
the kind one, slips a note
into my hand, whispers,
She sent her love. Back in my cell
I unfold a note that says,
Te amo, siempre in crude letters
formed by a finger and menstrual blood.

THE RAINLOCKER

Here, in the exquisite privacy of white
tile, curtains, and chrome,
something in the spray
of warm water against skin, the soap
reaming from forehead to toe
and back again, evokes
the unattainable—we are,
here, after all
manly men—
who only in seclusion,
in shower shoes and steam
without witness, can fully
surrender to the need for touch
that draws the hands
to the sexual root, the lathered
shorthairs of the chest and abdomen.
As if tending ourselves
with a little fingerplay, rain, and solitude
could allow a few moments
to bloom through the prison walls
the way grass and flowers
can erupt through stone, where
in a wild drive for the intimate
the unguarded spirit jets for home.

THE WEIGHT

Alice says we're marionettes
who once jerked about on the whims
of the Holy One until Lenin had the Bolsheviks
snip our strings. And now
on the western shore of the Atlantic
they're controlling our minds
with radio waves. A concept
more interesting than powdered eggs,
decaf coffee, the two hundred yellowing
tiles of the day room. Sometimes

she claims the staff
slip aphrodisiacs into the orange
drink or cough syrup, and asks
that I make sure she keeps her hands
to herself, although I try to convince her
they don't want us to multiply.
Seven years she's haunted
these rooms and halls, the green
vinyl chairs and couches, her skin
shiny from the ersatz light, tobacco smoke
and state soap. It's grown easier
for us both to pass the hours
talking by the window
rather than attempt the evening walks

or significance. Last night
she read to me from André Breton's
Young Cherry Trees Secured Against Hares
and told me she'd love to ride
the bed as it raced the changing skies
of blue honey. I can hear
her distant laugh in the Seclusion Room.
Whenever they take her I grab
hold of the wooden chair arms, plant
my feet on the floor
because always it feels like I'm falling.

BARRIO ANITA, 1983

for Frank Franklin

The low, Sonoran adobes along Anita Street
this evening, are coarse,
porous blocks, like sandstone,
that absorb the orange tint
of this desert twilight,
their deep-cut windows, screen door,
showing partial furniture, faces, lamplight.
Ahead, a Chicana girl, her belly
round against her shirt, pushes a boy
in a borrowed grocery cart, like a tiny convict,
past dirt yards littered with old bikes
and tricycles, frail fences
braided with grass, blue altars of the Virgin
holding flowers or doves—here,
things speak of growth
through pain, of patience and devotion.
Once, a friend here laughed
and told me his neighbor, *Gordo,*
when he was a drug-dealer, got in a fight with his wife
and stormed out the door
in his baggy *chollo* pants, moneybox
in hand, when she hit him from behind on the ass
with a two by four, his trousers
falling around his feet as she snagged the box
and fled down the street, never to return,
leaving him to drift between *Coronas*
and grief. But he's found Jesus now, visits
the jail on Sundays to listen, testify
and preach. Stopping to open
my friend's rusty gate, I can see him
in white shorts and T-shirt, leaning against
a post on the porch, the welcome glint
from his eyes and teeth enough
to light one country in the continent of my week.

EVENING PROFILE, TUCSON

A deep blue powders
the dusk sky as I stand
on the lawn, a friend's young
daughter pointing out the moon
and stars from her perch
on my shoulder, the blossoming
orange trees and fresh-

clipped grass forming
a kind of musk
that removes fear, when
from an airfield
in the city's southeast,
three camouflaged jets
ascend through the air, engines
screaming as they fold up
their landing gear.

Airplanes! she cries,
pulling at strands of my hair,
as if everything to navigate the sky
were friendly, magical,
dependent on our belief
to hold it up, whether it be
hawks, the moon and stars,
or the machines
that bear devices for dying.

GREY FIGURES

Not sixty miles from Mexico, father,
and I've learned only enough Spanish
to understand if I'm being insulted.
Here, the orange buildings of the prison
rise like hotels from the desert,
its dry tide of mesquite
and cholla like a green sea
around the fence, and for some
years now, I've called this

home. Sometimes, when I close
my eyes, it's easy
to imagine this
a small town, a village
in a foreign country—
through the vent grille
I can hear two Chicanos talking
about low-riders, wine,
a woman who undid everything
but her blue stockings
in the back of a car.
I live with these men, father;
like anywhere
some are my friends. Others
could die and I wouldn't notice.

But sometimes I want to repeat
my vow about building
a house on the edge of the forest
until we both believe it
possible, to tell you
that this time I'll make you
proud, repay every theft
of your hope—anything
but this fog that rises
like a beast from the ground

and obscures the figures of men
and stone, this small
seductive cloud that widens
to receive us
into its shallow, comforting dark.

REUNIONS

I finish reading my last poem   under soft auditorium lights
to a polite smattering of hands   when by the reception table
swigging cider   lifting slices from tiny coffins of banana bread
a skinhead in sleeveless black T-shirt   disappointed
tells me   that I look like the inspiration for *Doonsbury*
Someone asks if I ever knew Bob   X from New Mexico
the genius love poet   and import-export agent
recently found floating   face down in the Rio Grande
I shake hands with a New Yorker   who invites me
to share some cough syrup   he just brought from Jaurez
a man with taped-together glasses   shuffles forward to tell me
we should never be ashamed to be mentally ill   that we're in great company
and as the cider disappears   and the audience drifts away like smoke
I hear from some shadows   near the restroom
a raspy half-familiar voice   say *c'mere kid*
something like a sap smacking a hand   amidst a bouquet of wine and garlic
how it is a pleasure to find me   again after all these years
that the limo is across the street   and I'm going for a moonlight swim

WINTER IN MARYLAND

All winter, the snow shining,
I walked to school
through sharp holly and pine,
hoping this phase of my life
would soon be over, aware
that while teachers were useless
they were evils necessary
to please my parents
and the truant officer.

Now, though the pleading
and beatings have long since
stopped, and the nuns
packed off with good riddance
to atolls in the Pacific,
shacks on the Amazon
or New York, I would rather
have remained a child
than to grow up, armed with math
and philosophy, in a world

where the only path to wisdom
seems the one I have not yet traveled.

SARAH

The blackberries hung blood dark
from the vines near Foxhill Lake, our fingers
stained from the pints we plucked and brought
Mrs. Gill, who cooked them
to a thick jam she gave
everyone she liked. And sometimes
Sarah, five years
older than I, but slow,
would pull me by the hand
up the bare pine steps to her room,
lock the door, and undress for me
slowly to her white slip
and brassiere, standing warm
in the bright squares of windowlight,
lifting my hands to her face
and breast. Mornings, I'd watch her
board a yellow bus, shorter than mine,
for a special school
outside town. But she could
pick berries, run, and smile
more quickly than I,
and if she spoke or thought
more slowly, it was still
in the same language,
and those of us who knew her
listened, because
she was one of us, awake and alive.

BICYCLE MESSENGER

Perched in my toeclips
near the White House, drunk
on the April mix
of cherry blossoms, tourists,
ivy greening old buildings
and galleries, the sky
not yet a haze
of car exhaust, I arched my back
over the saddle
and noticed a woman
in a green blouse, her teeth
and eyes nearly obscured
by an auburn nimbus
of sun through hair, smiling
at me from the sidewalk.
Excuse me, she said, stepping
closer to the curb.
I thought I should tell you
there's bird shit on your shoulder.
The light turned, and she flipped
her hand in a wave. Laughing,
I pressed my bike into traffic,
toward the rain clouds
moving north over the Potomac.
Let me have it, I yelled to the sky.

MEETING IN SOUTH TUCSON

Because the squad car slows
to follow us down South Sixth Avenue,
she asks if I don't mind
taking her hand to pose
as her boyfriend. She slips
an arm around my waist, hooking
her fingers through a belt-loop
and pocket, even
after I know the police
have split and we've turned

down an alley fenced
by ocotillo shafts and oleander,
where shepherds and pit
bulls rage against their chains.
We stop at the milkcrate step
of an aluminum Airstream
where she knocks, meets the eyes
that check our faces
from behind the window blind.

Inside we clear a patch
of rug among some dirty jackets
as he cuts our gram
of heroin in foil. After the rituals
of cotton and water, she faces the window,
opening her blouse to expose
a small, Latin breast, asking
shyly, syringe in hand,
if I could find a vein there,
for no others are left.

Outside, eyelids
heavy, foreheads prickly with sweat
in the bright desert air,

she kisses my cheek,
and pursing her lips, writes
her name in black ink
on my wrist, so I don't forget.

EXILES

This is the last outpost
before the mountains rise uncharted
and rivers run black and deep as mystery;
the last time you will see the dawnlight
smoke through your curtains and curl
at the edge of your bed.
The last time you can numb yourself
with wine, prop your feet
before the warm, red stones
of the fireplace
and sleep your easy sleep.
        Beyond these gates
you will travel alone
with no one to bind your wounds
or guide you. Most who pass here
spend weeks wandering
the vast fields and forest
where crows perch like sentinels
on the limbs. Some few
have returned, weeping and pounding
the gates, offering anything
for another chance
inside. Of the others
we have heard nothing.
        So, my friend,
when we watch you
recede as you shove through the brush,
we know your past
will snake quietly after you,
that you may pick it up
and follow it back.
But I hope you keep going,
find the country you're searching for,

that if you arrive there
you build a house large enough
to hold many, and keep its windows
shining, my friend,
for us who long to follow.

THE TREEHOUSE

It was along the B&O tracks
my ninth October, the musk of creosote, spilled
train oil and coal
rising from the railbed, I described,
ecstatic, my dream treehouse
to the man I'd just met. How it would start
a platform in a great, grey oak
with insulated plywood walls, windows
whose shutters I could latch
in rain or winter, a slanted roof
weatherproofed with tar and shingles
stout enough to stand on.
A rope ladder I could raise or lower
for myself or guest.
He listened, finger to his lip, pushing
up the horn bridge of his glasses
as he interrupted to add
possible chairs, a small table
and bed, reciting
the list of materials we'd need,
most of it hand tools
and wood he kept in a shed.
We could meet
afternoons, after last period
at school, by the oak
we chose in the forest. We stopped
on the tiny bridge over Collington Creek
where he said something
about how free, clear water
always triggered a need in him
to take a leak. *It's like that for us men,*
he said, slapping my back,
and as we both finished tinting the stream
he slipped one hand in my zipper, the other
along my ass. Something in me
exchanged fear for the greater good:

the refuge in the trees, silence and solitude.
Worse was the boy I became
all winter, ready to forgive all,
if not forget, an eye cocked on the tracks,
if only he would pick up his tools and come back.

NATURAL KNOWLEDGE

As an amputee remembers
the touch of a missing limb,
so the charred stumps of this field
remember their trees.

Where this forest once stood,
its trunks tall as a long rain,
the birds recall its branches
and sing as they weave between them.

NOTES ON THE POEMS

Miklos Radnoti was a Hungarian poet forced into slave labor by the Nazis. His body, along with his last poems, was found by his wife in a mass grave.

René Magritte. Several poems here have titles directly or indirectly stolen from his work.

Barrio Anita is located in west-central Tucson.

Siempre. Anyone familiar with state prisons and jails knows it is rare for women and men to be housed close to one another; this situation did exist, however (and perhaps still does), in the Pima County Jail Psych Unit. The "train" referred to here is prisoner slang for any transport going to the prison system.